PRESENTED TO

_____

BY

_____

_____

Psalm 126:6

Rejoice, You're a Sunday School Teacher!

John T. Sisemore

Broadman Press/Nashville, Tennessee

ILLUSTRATIONS BY RON HESTER

© Copyright 1977 • Broadman Press

4251-47
ISBN: 0-8054-5147-1

Subject headings: SUNDAY SCHOOLS//TEACHING
Dewey Decimal Classification: 268.3
Library of Congress Catalog Card Number: 76-20053
Printed in the United States of America

Dedication

As a general practice this writer does not dedicate books to individuals. However, it seems quite appropriate that this work be dedicated to an inspiring personification of a truly joyful teacher—Margaret Sisemore. She is a teacher of great ability who writes no books. Her husband-author simply observes her happy performance and records what he sees. And it is his joy to share the experience with others.

Preface

If you are a Sunday School teacher, this book is about you and for you!

It is not a "how-to" book on teaching. It does not deal with teaching philosophy, methods, techniques, curriculum, materials, equipment, or space. Rather, it focuses on the teacher's attitude toward teaching, the call to teach, the prerequisites for teaching, and the content to be taught. There is also an emphasis on the day-by-day joy of teaching, the role of the Holy Spirit in teaching, the ultimate results in teaching, and God's tribute to teachers.

Few Sunday School teachers will ever reach their full potential until they become excited about teaching people the Bible. And excitement is an emotional response to a challenge that has been personally experienced and accepted.

Obviously there is no motivational excitement when there is no challenge, or when there is no perception of a challenge which actually exists. Hopefully, both the challenge and the excitement of teaching are woven into the fabric of this book.

Simply stated, the overarching objective of this book is to inspire and strengthen the *desire* to teach. This purpose makes the book a why-to volume on teaching. Such a concept is an all but unexplored area in Christian writing.

A more precise statement of purpose is to help you as

a teacher of God's Word to find a new and fresh motivation to become the most effective teacher you are capable of becoming. Also, it is my hope that this work will help you experience that greatest of all joys—helping others grow through Bible study into all that God wants them to become.

While you read, and after you have finished reading this book, it is my very sincere prayer that you be stimulated to "Rejoice, you're a Sunday School teacher!"

Contents

1
Rejoice in Your Heritage

Both of the men were weeping as they walked arm-in-arm to the front of the sanctuary. When the pastor greeted them, one of the men seemed to alternate between tears of grief and tears of relief. The other man's face, even as he wept, seemed to radiate an unmistakable expression of intense happiness. Quite obviously this man was a Sunday School teacher who was experiencing the *ultimate* joy. He was one of those who had "come again with rejoicing, bringing his sheaves with him" (Ps. 126:6).

One of the most awesome and joy-filled responsibilities a Sunday School teacher has is helping unsaved persons become Christians. His assignments of teaching and witnessing put him in an enviable position. It is a position of finding, relating to, and bringing unsaved persons face-to-face with Christ.

When these persons experience salvation, the teacher has come to his finest hour. It is a time of *indescribable* joy. Nothing else can compare with the elation which comes from sharing in the salvation of another person. It may even be a greater joy than that which comes with our own personal salvation. Why? Because we have become an instrument in God's redeeming grace. This is the meaning of John's statement "that our joy may be complete" (1 John 1:4, RSV).

But there are many additional causes for rejoicing which

come to the teacher simply because he is a *teacher*. So, if you are now a teacher, or if you are contemplating becoming one, congratulations are in order! Many matchless experiences await you—experiences which will give you sufficient cause to rejoice always. And this entire book is devoted to helping you realize the full range of all these experiences.

Teaching Is Time-Honored

Let's begin with a look at your position as a teacher. It is an honorable and a notable position, one of distinction and prominence. Thousands of others share that title with you. Although there has never been any effort made to organize Sunday School teachers into a united force, this group now constitutes the world's largest and most influential corps of volunteer educators.

Present-day churches and their pastors would find it all but impossible to function without the aid of the Sunday School teachers. However, it has not always been so. The position of Sunday School teacher has existed for only two hundred years. The real significance of the teacher has developed largely in the past half century.

Nevertheless, the title *teacher* in its relation to the communication of religious truth is far from new. The concept of teaching and the role of the teacher are of ancient origin. They are much older than the Sunday School and even antedate the church itself. As far back as 2500 B.C., there were formal schools and professional teachers in the various cultures of the Near East. These schools were probably the fountainhead of the educational flow so prominent in the early Hebrew practice of religious education.

Teaching Is a Concomitant of Religion

If you were to review the very earliest historical data available, you would find teaching as the central channel in the stream of religious concerns. Wherever and whenever there has been religion, there also has been teaching. This fact is amply illustrated in Judaism. Even though formal schools were rather late in arriving in the Hebrew culture (between 75 B.C. and A.D. 64), there was a strong reliance on teaching. For hundreds of years before Christ the Jews carried on a most effective teaching program in which religious instruction was an integral part of personal, family, and community life.

Teaching enjoyed an especially prominent role in the daily routine of the Hebrew family. Teachings about God, religious rites, and moral codes were first learned in the family setting. These teachings were an essential part of the religious ceremonies that were practiced in the Hebrew home.

As a teacher and an adult, you will be pleased to know that in the early developments of the educational systems of the Jewish faith, adults were not overlooked. They not only taught their own family; they were learners themselves. There is a long line of priests, prophets, seers, sages, poets, and scribes who were teachers of the adult generation.

This emphasis on adult education was not an incidental part of the Hebrew culture. It was essential because the *teachers* needed to be taught. There was also an element of divine strategy involved. On several occasions, God himself commanded the leaders to gather the people together for instruction (see Deut. 4:10; 31:11-13).

After the exile of Judah, teaching became more formalized. The synagogue as an institution developed as the center of a worship-type learning. Its primary purpose was to educate the people in and through religious services. These services were largely instructional in nature.

Out of the Jews' desire to teach their people, three other formal schools evolved. These schools were related but distinct in their own right. They were essentially elementary, secondary, and academy approaches to teaching. Each of these schools was religious in nature, but the academy had overtones of a university, seminary, research center, and even a supreme court.

Are you aware that in Christianity, as in its parent Judaism, there is an obvious dynamic that makes teaching necessary? This compelling force grows out of the missionary nature of the Christian religion. Furthermore, the most striking characteristic of Christianity is the master-disciple (teacher-learner) relationship which it magnifies. These forces have propelled teaching into the forefront of all Christian endeavors.

Teaching Is Prominent in the Scriptures

You are familiar enough with Old Testament Scriptures to know that they are rich in their descriptions of the teacher and the work of the teacher. For example, the books of the Law required all Israel and their leaders to teach the Scriptures to their children. The historical books of the Old Testament contain many statements about the necessity of teaching. The books of poetry, especially the Psalms, are rich in their references to the significance and value of teaching. The prophetic books recognize the importance of teaching. Isaiah beautifully described it as "precept upon precept; . . . line upon line; here a little, and there a little" (Isa. 28:10).

Old Testament Scriptures frequently prescribe the content of teaching, the methodology for teaching, the situation of teaching, the purposes in teaching, and even the individuals to be taught. These Scriptures also point out the blessings that come when teaching is heeded, or the eventual result if it is ignored. They praise the faithful teacher, and they pronounce woe upon the unfaithful teacher.

In the area of Judaism there was no position as exalted as that of the teacher. The rabbi was the most honored and revered person in the community. He was the official instructor and the interpreter of the Holy Scriptures. To question his authority or to show any kind of disrespect for him was considered essentially as sinful as discrediting God.

As strong as the teaching emphasis is in the Old Testament, the New Testament places a far greater emphasis upon it. Except for the emphasis on evangelism and the personal life of the Christian, there is no more dominant theme in the Bible than that of teaching. And there is no position more respected or honored than that of the one you hold—*teacher.*

Teaching Was Central in Jesus' Ministry

Throughout the Gospels Jesus is repeatedly referred to and addressed as "Teacher" or an equivalent title. Sixty times he is called "Rabbi." In about thirty other instances he is called "Master" *(didaskalos)* which means a person who taught the things of God and the duties of man. Identification with the Master Teacher places you, a Sunday School teacher, in a noble line.

Apparently Jesus approved of the fact that the people regarded him primarily as a teacher. In 143 passages he is referred to as preacher, but in 217 he is alluded to as teacher. There is no record that he objected to either title, but he seemed to view himself primarily as a teacher.

Frequently the phrases "he taught in their synagogues" (Luke 4:15), and he "taught them saying" (Matt. 5:2), occur in the Gospels. In John 13:13 he said to the disciples: "You call me Teacher and Lord; and you are right; for so I am" (NASB).

Jesus taught at every possible opportunity. He taught in every possible way. He taught on almost all subjects of interest to the people of his day. He graced and dignified the position of teacher far beyond anything that Plato, Socrates, and Aristotle combined could ever do. Jesus was so effective as a teacher that Nicodemus said to him "Rabbi, we know that you have come from God as a teacher" (John 3:2, NASB).

Wherever Jesus taught, huge crowds gathered and listened in rapt attention. These crowds eagerly asked questions, and he responded to their questions in a loving and careful manner. Friends and enemies alike were attracted by his teaching ability. It was readily acknowledged that he taught in a most unusual manner—"as one having authority" (Matt. 7:29).

Jesus dedicated most of his earthly ministry to teaching, especially to teaching the disciples. His teaching was so effective that it distracted the people from their daily routines, disturbed the professional theological experts, and dismayed the Roman government.

In Jesus' final instructions to his disciples, he included an especially strong emphasis on teaching. In his final commission to his church, he linked to teaching both the beginning and the continuing aspects of the gospel. He placed teaching at the heart of the discipling process. He promised his continuing presence to those who obeyed him by teaching and training those who had been won. Obviously teaching held a most significant place in the strategy of Christ, as well as in his ministry here on earth.

Teaching Was Vital to Early Christians

The apostles were caught up in the enthusiasm for teaching which Jesus seemed to exude. Peter was especially effective as a teacher. In his work as a teacher he infuriated the Jewish council as well as the high priests in Jerusalem. These leaders became so frightened at his teaching expertise that they arrested and imprisoned him.

After they had put him in prison, the prison doors were miraculously opened. Rather than escape, Peter remained in prison. These circumstances so unnerved the Jewish officials that they said to Peter, "We gave you strict orders not to continue teaching in this name, and, behold, you have filled Jerusalem with your teaching" (Acts 5:28, NASB).

Peter and the other apostles were so convincing in their defense before the council that the council decided it was best to destroy them. Had it not been for Gamaliel's logic, these apostles could well have become the first martyrs. And they would have been martyred for their expertise in teaching! After the apostles were warned again and beaten by the council, they returned immediately to teaching and preaching Jesus Christ.

In Acts 13, Luke made it clear that recognized men in the church at Antioch were known as teachers. Included among those listed in the chapter are men of great stature—Barnabas and Paul in particular. Apparently the major ability of these men and others like them was their skill in instructing and guiding others as they tried to understand and learn to live the Christian faith.

As the gospel spread to the Gentiles, teaching seemed to become even more important in the communication of the good news and in the interpretation of what it produced. Teaching, therefore, became the essence of the work of the leaders, especially of the renowned Paul. His teaching was known throughout the New Testament world. And because of his effectiveness, the teaching of the gospel was held in high esteem. This fact is all the more unique when it is remembered that the Roman Empire was known more for its ability in war and battle than for its intellectual interests.

In the present-day church, you and other Sunday School teachers occupy an extremely strategic place. Your role is so vital it is hard to believe that churches have not always had your services.

Teaching Is the Contemporary Thrust

Can you imagine what a church—your church—would be like without a Sunday School? Can you imagine how a Sunday School could function without dedicated and capable teachers?

The marvel of the church today is what God is doing through persons who work on a voluntary basis, who voluntarily enlist class members, and who guide these members in a voluntary study of the Bible.

It is not a disparagement of any other church program or leader to say that the Sunday School and its teachers are the very essence of a church at work in outreach, Bible teaching, evangelism, and ministry. Nor is there any doubt that Sunday School teachers have become the most productive team in a church, regardless of its size, location, or constituency.

The word *rejoice* is used frequently in the New Testament. Many reasons for rejoicing, many occasions for rejoicing, and many forms of rejoicing are revealed, especially in relation to the blessings of the Christian life and service.

The Greek word for rejoice *(chairo)* can also mean to exult, to make merry, to gladden, to glory, and to boast. The word undoubtedly implies that a Christian worker of any kind should be positive, happy, and even exuberant in the Lord. This idea is exactly what Paul had in mind when he wrote: "Always be full of joy in the Lord; I say it again, rejoice!" (Phil. 4:4, TLB).

This verse, a quotation from Psalm 37:4, does not in its immediate context relate to Bible teaching, but it is not unrelated by any means. Over a period of time there is no form of Christian service that provides more cause for rejoicing than the service of teaching. The privilege of being a partner with God in helping persons learn the Scriptures, understand their meaning, and shape their lives by biblical truth is a rare privilege indeed. It is one that should cause you to "always be full of joy."

So, rejoice, Sunday School teacher! You follow in the steps of a mighty and magnificent line of Christian servants, Christian leaders, Christian churchmen, and above all, Christian teachers.

2
Called to Teach

How did you become a Sunday School teacher? The pastor begged you? The Sunday School director bugged you? The minister of education bribed you? Ridiculous as it may seem, there are some teachers who have no more awareness of a sense of "call" to teach than these questions indicate.

Once while serving as a minister of education, I was approached by a man who said, "I'd like to have a class to teach." Because the man did not seem to have any sense of call or commitment to teaching, I asked him why he wanted to teach. The response was unbelievable: "I am enrolled in a public speaking class at the university. The professor said I had 'a gift for gab' and I need a place to exercise it."

All Christians Are Called

Kaleō is the beautiful Greek verb which means *invite, call,* or *summon.* The invitation, the call, the summons carry an implied purpose. In the Christian context, the purpose is obviously a call to salvation and service. The nature of this word is such that the call is either an appeal or a challenge. It can be accepted, or it can be rejected; but it requires a response.

If you are a Christian, God has called you once, yea, twice, or in two ways. The Bible teaches that the Christian is first called of God to redemption. It also teaches that the Christian is called to service, that is, to servantship.

Each person who responds to the call of God becomes a part of the priesthood of which Christ is the High Priest (Heb. 4:14). As a member of the royal priesthood, the believer becomes a minister *(diakonos)*. This word does not refer to position, rank, or station. It means a servant or attendant who is responsible for service-type functions both for his Master and for others.

This brief summary of the doctrine of the priesthood of the believer simply underscores the fact that all Christians are truly called to be ministers (servants) to serve both within and outside the church membership.

God Calls to Specific Tasks

When God called Abraham, probably the first person to receive a specific call from God, to participate in his eternal purpose, Abraham responded positively. He left his home and country without knowing where God had called him to go. God called Hosea, and he became a prophet of divine love. God called Amos, and he served as a prophet of social righteousness. God called Moses to be the national and religious leader of Israel. God called Elijah, Samuel, Isaiah, Jeremiah, and many other persons to be prophets, each one with his special work among God's people.

In the Gospels, Jesus is seen calling numerous persons to follow him and to serve alongside him. Paul was called to be an apostle to the Gentiles. Not only were individuals called to a particular task, but God also called teammates into his service. Barnabas and Saul were called to do missionary work. Paul and Timothy were called to preach in Macedonia.

Throughout biblical history individuals called to serve God have carried a variety of titles. At least twenty-six different designations are used to identify the specialized areas of religious service.

Many of those who were called were of noble birth and persons of renown. There were kings, wise men, prophets, priests, scribes (writers and editors), and national leaders in the group. However, the true greatness of every one of these people is wrapped up in a phrase, service to God.

I find it inspiring to realize that God called numerous persons of unusual ability to serve him. But it is easy to overlook the fact that many of the people God called were very ordinary people—just like most of the Sunday School teachers in your church and mine. In the Williams translation of 1 Corinthians 1:26-29, Paul points up this fact:

> For consider, brothers, the way God called you; that not many of you, in accordance with human standards, were wise, not many influential, not many of high birth. Just the opposite: God chose what the world calls foolish to put the wise to shame, what the world calls weak to put the strong to shame, what the world calls of low degree, yea, what it counts as nothing and what it thinks does not exist . . . so that no mortal man might ever boast in the presence of God.

Most of the members of the church at Corinth were not a part of the "upper-middle-class" of the population. It is likely that they were from the very lowest class. Paul's frequent references to boasting indicate that they were also overly self-reliant and self-confident. They needed to be reminded that humility is essential to service for God.

Just as Christians should avoid pride in their service

they should also refrain from excessive self-effacement. A truly humble-minded person is quite likely to be aware of his personal limitations, but every Christian needs to remember that human limitation is undergirded by divine power.

A balance between these two extremes of superpride and false humility is the ideal. Self-confidence without egotism and humility without self-conceit are most desirable. It is also helpful to remember that Christians do not have to be a power for God but that they ought to be a channel through which God's power can flow.

Teaching Is a Divine Call

In New Testament times the need for teaching was acute. Many of the early Christians had come directly from paganism. They needed to be instructed so they could become rooted and grounded in the faith. This important function was served by special persons who were probably some kind of officials in the churches. They were called teachers *(didaskalos)* and they had the responsibility of caring for, instructing, and guiding the less mature Christians in their growth. Living an exemplary life before those who were taught was considered an integral part of the teaching process.

In Ephesians 4:11 Paul makes it clear that God's calling individuals to the ministry of teaching met the need of the early churches and present-day churches by calling them—just as surely as he calls some to the pastoral ministry, to the work of evangelism, or to missionary service.

The teaching ministry is specifically assigned the task of perfecting and equipping the saints so they could build up the body of Christ, the church. Some interpreters believe that the grammatical structure in Ephesians 4 assigns the edifying task to the pastor in his role as a teacher. Obviously such an assignment is inherent in the pastoral ministry. But why two different titles for just one function? And why are prophets linked with teachers in Acts 13:1? And why are prophets and teachers listed separately in 1 Corinthians 12:28? And why are both pastors and evangelists omitted from the Corinthian listing?

Apparently teachers were a separate group of ministers, even though their function was sometimes combined with other functions and sometimes performed by other leaders just as all the other ministries were from time to time. At any rate, in the first-century church, teaching was a specific ministry, the teacher was a central figure, and the persons who held the office were divinely called to teach.

The ascended Lord gave the gift of teaching to those whom he desired; he assigned those whom he had thus endowed to specific churches; and he so blessed their ministry that the civilized world was Christianized in three hundred years. Such is the fruit of teaching that God manifestly intended from persons he called to be teachers.

A Call to Teach May Be Verified

How does a person receive a call from God? Is there some certain experience or feeling? Is there an audible voice speaking to the individual? Is there some physical or psychic phenomenon involved?

These are certainly appropriate questions, but they are far easier to ask than to answer. Anyone would be hard pressed even to define a "call" in a simple way. And the manner in which it comes is even more difficult to explain.

One thing seems certain: there is no uniformity in the experience of being called. God seems to honor the uniqueness of the personality, temperament, and disposition of the persons he has created by dealing with each one differently. It is probably safe to say that God seldom, if ever, speaks audibly to a person in this day when he issues a call to teach.

The Scriptures indicate that some persons had unusual experiences when God called. Saul was struck blind by a great light at noontime. Moses found an inescapable challenge at Mount Horeb, but Elijah heard only a "still small voice" on that same mountain. Others simply experienced an awareness of God's need for them and found a willingness to respond.

It is not likely that a person today will be called to be a Sunday School teacher by some startling sign or phenomenon. Nor is it necessarily true that an individual who has a personal *need* to teach, *needs* to teach!

Let me share some of the more certain and assuring evidences of being the kind of *person* God may call to be a teacher:

1. A personal experience of faith in Jesus Christ as Savior;

2. A resolute and unapologetic commitment to Christ and the church, coupled with a desire to help others find that same quality of life;

3. A strong commitment to the Bible as the authoritative word of God and a desire to be involved in studying and sharing its riches;

4. A genuine concern for persons who are in obvious need of knowing and understanding the Bible;

5. An abiding sense of personal availability which makes the individual willing to accept a share of the hurt, sin, unbelief, and rebellion of unsaved and/or uncommitted persons;

6. A fundamental honesty that causes the individual to be trustworthy and dependable in the face of long-term responsibility;

7. A reasonable amount of natural ability for studying, planning, and working cooperatively with others;

8. A willingness to work at developing the innate talents which God has given, even though the individual may not realize he has such talents.

If a person does not have any or all of these qualities, can he be called to teach? Not necessarily, but possibly and even probably. Remember that when God called you to partake of the blessings of salvation, he also summoned you to service. Remember also that God has endowed every Christian with many "grace gifts"—gifts (charismata) which the Holy Spirit gives to every Christian, even though the gifts may still be undiscovered, undeveloped, and unused.

In the New Testament there are five separate listings of the gifts of the Spirit, plus a number of other isolated references to spiritual gifts. In these listings there is a total of seventeen different gifts of the Spirit. In each of the five listings (Rom. 12:6-8; 1 Cor. 12:4-10; 1 Cor. 12:28-30; Eph. 4:11; and 1 Pet. 4:10-11) the gift of teaching is found in some form. It is the *only* gift included in all five listings. These facts seem to point up the prominence of the teaching gift, and the many functions to which teaching relates.

But how about the call to teach? "Do I have it?" you may be asking. If you enjoy reading, maybe. If you enjoy studying, possibly. If you explain things well, likely. If you enjoy organizing and relating ideas, probably. If you get excited about helping people learn, absolutely! Why? Because these qualities are inherently a part of the didactically gifted person, and they are likely to characterize the "called teachers" God has given to the churches.

It seems biblically sound to believe that you may know by some reassuring confirmation of the Holy Spirit that you are called to teach. At least three times the apostle Paul wrote that he had been called to be an apostle, a preacher, and a teacher. Because Paul related no phenomenal experience concerning the certainty of his threefold call, we can only assume that he was assured of it by the Holy Spirit. We do not know how this affirmation came. It may have been only a growing feeling of God's assistance in his work and a sense of divine blessing on his ministry. At any rate, almost every teacher who seems to feel God's call to teach has this feeling of confirmation from time to time, if not permanently.

The feeling may at times be one of deep satisfaction that God is using you to help others. At other times it may be only a longing to be more and do more for your class members. At least on occasions, there could be a psychological uplift, and even a physical thrill, that cannot be explained except that God is affirming you as his servant. Even in those "off days" when things seem to be almost hopeless, there can still be the "blessed assurance" of "perfect submission" to God's will. That is affirmation! If you have not had some of these experiences as a teacher, there may be room to doubt the reality of having been called to teach.

Probably an opportunity to serve, an interest in teaching, and a feeling that the Lord wants you to teach are basic evidences of a call to teach. A growing sense of fulfillment and joy in the work would likely be a confirming act of the Holy Spirit.

Teaching is an open avenue of service to the Lord, the church, and the class members. Being able to help persons grow in Christlikeness is a joyful challenge, and it is wonderfully reassuring to know that He gave some to be teachers (see Eph. 4:11).

In this chapter we have spoken about God's call to salvation, to service, and to teaching. The following poetic lines express not only my personal viewpoint but also my earnest desire.

"God's Call"

God's call is a wonderful thing!
  It's a call to salvation free;
Through the gift of his own dear Son,
  His love was extended to me.

God's call is a wonderful thing!
  It's a call to walk in his way;
With joyful heart I'll seek his will,
  And follow him come what may.

God's call is a wonderful thing!
  It's a call to serve him each day;
With the gifts which his grace bestowed,
  I'll do what he wants in his way.

—JOHN T. SISEMORE

3
Worthy of the Calling

Is there a Sunday School teacher life-style? Is there some special or particular level of living that is required simply because an individual is a Sunday School teacher? Are there positive qualities of life that a teacher should develop? Are there negative activities in which a teacher should not participate?

Is the life-style of a Sunday School teacher to be dictated by adherence to or avoidance of some arbitrary standards? Does a teacher's liberty in Christ make him free from all guidelines or requirements in his personal way of life? Is the quality of a Sunday School teacher's belief more important than the quality of his behavior? Are there principles by which a teacher may live that are more scriptural than some prescribed rules and regulations that are produced by a committee or even a church?

These questions bring to mind a question that was raised by the apostle Peter, "What manner of persons ought ye to be?" (2 Pet. 3:11).

In discussing the kind of person a "called" worker should be, Paul said, "I therefore, the prisoner of the Lord, entreat you to walk in a manner worthy of the calling with which you have been called" (Eph. 4:1, NASB). The word *walk* has an interesting background in the Scriptures. For example, Enoch is said to have "walked with God" (Gen. 5:22). First John 2:6 states clearly that "he who says he abides

in him ought to walk in the same way in which he walked"
(RSV).

These illustrations indicate that *walk* refers more to the
course of one's life than to the primal mode of trans-
portation. In current terminology, *walk* means a life-style
that is in harmony with God's holy calling. The word *holy,*
among other things, means different. Thus, a holy calling
is one that is different both in kind and quality from any
other vocation or avocation. To summarize this truth, it
is biblically accurate to say that the Christian, especially
one who is a Sunday School teacher, has a responsibility
to live differently (in holiness) because he is a different
person with a different perspective and a different purpose
in life.

As far as I can determine, there is no universally accepted conduct norm to which a Christian or a Sunday
School teacher must slavishly conform. But, it would be
sheer folly to think that there are no specific elements
which distinguish a Christian from the non-Christian, or
even a Sunday School teacher from the "typical" church
member.

Everyone who has read the New Testament, even in
a cursory fashion, knows that the Scriptures contain numerous statements about what God expects of his people.
For example, in Romans 12 there are approximately thirty
different admonitions, both positive and negative, regarding the Christian life-style. Note some of the far-ranging
admonitions Paul mentioned (excerpts from NASB):

"Present your bodies a living and holy sacrifice" (v. 1);

"Do not be conformed to this world" (v. 2);

"Not to think more highly of himself than he ought
to think" (v. 3);

"Since we have gifts that differ . . . let each exercise

them accordingly" (v. 6);

"Let love be without hypocrisy. Abhor what is evil; cleave to what is good. Be devoted to one another . . . give preference to one another" (vv. 9-10);

"Not lagging behind in diligence, fervent in spirit" (v. 11);

"Devoted to prayer" (v. 12);

"Bless those who persecute you" (v. 14);

"Rejoice with those who rejoice, and weep with those who weep" (v. 15);

"Do not be wise in your own estimation" (v. 16);

"Be at peace with all men" (v. 18);

"Overcome evil with good" (v. 21).

Would you agree that the qualities represented in these reminders should be a part of the teacher's life-style? If so, would you make a personal commitment to develop these traits? The approach suggested in the remainder of this chapter is one you may wish to follow.

Reflect Christ

Walking worthy of the call to teach begins with the decision to reflect Christ. There is something truly unique about the genuine Christian and his way of life. The anti-Christian world recognized this uniqueness. It was said of Peter and John that "they took knowledge of them, that they had been with Jesus" (Acts 4:13). These two men had shown themselves to be patient but persistent in their teaching. They were firm but felicitous in their message. They were surprised but steadfast in their mission. They were persecuted but poised in their arraignment. They were condemned but confident in their predicament. They were uniquely different.

The steady faith, the serene fortitude, and the sensible

finesse of Peter and John did not come from their culture or education. These things were theirs because they had walked with and learned from the Master Teacher. Their life-style was a reflection of Christ.

Jesus apparently had a pattern of life in mind for all of his followers when he said: "I have set you an example that you should do as I have done" (John 13:15, NIV). Peter recognized this desire of Jesus when he wrote: "For you have been called for this purpose, since Christ also suffered for you, leaving you an example for you to follow in His steps" (1 Pet. 2:21, NASB).

This new kind of life-style which Jesus had in mind was not some vague set of philosophical propositions nor was it a set of stereotyped standards to be mechanically followed. It was a tangible, identifiable, assessable level of living. It was the pattern which Jesus set as the Son of God, the kind of life which God expects of every Christian in his personal behavior. It is not a kind of life that is required even by God's law. It is one which comes as a result of the new life in Christ and which is the possession of every true believer. In other words, the teacher's pattern of life is (1) A matter of *relationship*—"Christ in you," (Col. 1:27); (2) a matter of *reflection*—"walk in a manner worthy of the Lord" (v. 10, NASB); (3) a matter of *replication*—"do as I have done" (John 13:15).

Let the beauty of Jesus be seen in me,
All His wonderful passion and purity;
O Thou Spirit divine,
All my nature refine,
Till the beauty of Jesus be seen in me.

—ALBERT ORSBORN

Be a Moral Example

Peter provided keen insight into what being a moral example involves: "Indeed, it was to this kind of living that you were called, because Christ also suffered for you, leaving you an example that you might follow his footsteps" (1 Pet. 2:21, Williams).

The Greek word for "example" *(hupogrammos)* is used only this one time in the New Testament. The word has an educational background. It refers to the practice of the teacher in drawing pairs of parallel lines for the students to write between as they copied the perfect example which the teacher had written at the top of the wax tablets. Sometimes the teacher wrote the material on the tablet and held the pupil's hand as the pupil traced the letters with his stylus. In this way the pupil would make a perfect copy.

This illustration is probably what Peter had in mind when he taught that Christ had left an example so Christians could learn to live by copying the perfect life pattern of Jesus.

In the beautiful fourth and fifth chapters of Ephesians, Paul elaborates on the moral qualities of the life which "copies" the example of Jesus and makes the Christian an imitator of God. To read these chapters is both to thrill at the possibility of living like the example which Christ left, and to be humiliated because of the failure to do so.

Is it actually possible to be a moral example? Does this mean being perfect? Does it require sinlessness? No one is, or can be, perfect in all his behavior.

What is required is that the Christian bring his life under the lordship of Christ. This relationship puts the moral and immoral elements of life under divine tension. In this state of tension the morality of Christ brings the immorality of man under the focus of God's holy light. "If we walk in the light as He Himself is in the light, we have fellowship with one another, and the blood of Jesus His Son cleanses us from all sin" (1 John 1:7, NASB).

Probably the greatest problem in the moral conduct of a Christian is the notion that the Christian must live *for* Christ. *The real truth is that the Christian must allow Christ to live his life through the Christian.* Where Christ *dwells,* morality must abide. "It is quite true that the way to live a godly life is not an easy matter. But the answer lies in Christ" (1 Tim. 3:16, TLB).

Grow in Christian Personality

By virtue of his position, the Sunday School teacher is a person of importance and far-reaching influence. Therefore, what a teacher is as a personality, as well as what he is as a Christian, determines to a considerable degree the effectiveness of his teaching. The single most vital factor in the teacher's success is himself. This is because the quality of being a person is the essence of that elusive element known as personality.

Personality is the sum of all the factors in a person's being which influence other people. When that personality is reborn, directed by the Holy Spirit, and is becoming transformed into the likeness of Christ, it is the most significant element in the whole teaching-learning process. A teacher teaches some by what he says, more by what he does, and most by what he is.

When a Sunday School teacher realizes the pivotal role of his personality in the success of his teaching, he will become concerned about the need for improving his personality. Even though there is a hereditary aspect of personality that is largely fixed, it is a gross error to assume that personality cannot be improved. In fact, personality cannot remain constant, because it is always in the process of becoming what it is. Although a teacher is unable to change the ultimate boundaries of his personality, he is quite capable of cultivating, improving, and developing his personality within the boundaries which his heredity has given him.

The growing person begins his personality improvement program by accepting gracefully what he is—a unique individual made as God desired him to be—for His own glory. Building on this wholesome attitude, the teacher should make a reasonable effort to discover and understand his strengths and weaknesses, his assets and liabilities, his tendencies and his divergencies, his biases and his prejudices, his skills and his latent abilities. With the results of such a study the teacher is ready to take specific steps in an effort to polish his personality.

Although a person can make only a limited improvement in his physical appearance, he can take care of his health and thereby enhance the buoyancy of his personality which is so essential to effective work with other people. These vibrant signs of personality—energy, vigor, and vitality—are simply the evidence of a healthy body, an alert mind, and a spiritual reservoir.

Personality growth also must include special attention to the development of several mental qualities. Teachers need to give attention to objective thinking, sound judgment, mental alertness, creative imagination, and intensive concentration. Fortunately all of these qualities can be cultivated and increased.

A teacher may have the finest mental qualities and yet fail because of emotional and temperamental "raw edges."

Just the difference between a positive and a negative outlook is enough to disqualify many persons as teachers. Add to this attitudinal factor the many emotional traits such as love, friendliness, optimism, cheerfulness, sympathy, compassion, enthusiasm, sense of humor, courtesy, kindness, poise, and perseverance—and discover that there is much room for personality growth, even for the most winsome person.

When the teacher's personality becomes a product of divine energy, it is potentially greater than any curriculum, technique, or material used in the teaching-learning process. Becoming such a divinely endowed person is primarily a matter of "letting." Letting God's presence make you a better person, letting God's Spirit give you a more gracious and winsome manner, letting God's Word strengthen you for victory over temptation. Merely by "letting" you can release divine power when you yield yourself reverently and expectantly into God's gracious hands. He wants to make you far more effective as a personality than you have ever dreamed.

Without even considering the several other extremely important facets of personality, the physical, mental, emotional, and spiritual aspects presented thus far open vast areas of potential growth and development. The challenge these opportunities present is both an opportunity and a responsibility which every Sunday School teacher must face if he has the desire to walk worthy of his calling.

Develop Spiritual Sensitivity

Vague as it may seem, spirituality is the most important quality of the teacher who seeks to walk worthy of his calling. Spirituality may be defined in several ways. Here is one definition: a quality of life that is in harmony with the will of God, permeated by the love of Jesus, integrated with the power of the Holy Spirit, and occupied with the concerns of Christianity. This life is characterized by service, sacrifice, and sensitivity to the spiritual needs of persons—especially the ones who fall under the responsibility of the teacher's care.

Spirituality in this sense grows out of a heartsearching closeness to God and an attitude of dependence on the leadership of the Holy Spirit. It is based on a recognition of the lordship of Christ, and it is evaluated in terms of discipleship. Pity, sympathy, concern, care, love, compassion, and other such graces of the spirit are often observed in the character of the person who is spiritually sensitive. Effusive piosity is not necessarily a mark of a spiritual person. It could even be the evidence of spiritual pride. True spirituality is difficult to "put on." It is more likely to "ooze out" in a sensitivity to the deeper needs of persons.

The full meaning of spiritual sensitivity is difficult to comprehend. It probably includes the abandonment of everything that is self-oriented. Such matters as self-seeking, self-interest, self-serving, and self-centeredness are enemies of a sensitivity to the Holy Spirit's leadership and to the real needs of people. Jesus seemed to indicate that self-surrender to him was imperative in such a level of spiritual existence. "If anyone wishes to come after Me, let him deny [repudiate] himself, and take up his cross, and follow Me" (Matt. 16:24, NASB).

You have many strong points already. Magnify them! You have biblical evidence that others have walked worthy. Follow them! You have tremendous resources at your command. Use them! You have many promises that God will help you. Claim them! You have many fellow teachers who are walking worthily. Accompany them!

4
Teach These Truths

Holy Bible, Book Divine,
Precious treasure, thou art mine:
Mine to tell me whence I came;
Mine to teach me what I am.

Mine to chide me when I rove,
Mine to show a Savior's love;
Mine thou art to guide and guard;
Mine to punish or reward.

Mine to comfort in distress,
Suffr'ing in this wilderness;
Mine to show, by living faith,
Man can triumph over death.
—JOHN BURTON, SR.

God spells out clearly his magnificent purpose in giving us the Bible: "All Scripture is inspired by God and is useful for teaching the faith and correcting error, for resetting the direction of a man's life and training him in good living" (2 Tim. 3:16, Phillips).

This fourfold purpose is impossible to achieve without personal study, careful thought, and effective instruction. It follows then that knowing and understanding what God has revealed becomes highly involved with the educational

process, especially with teaching. The Sunday School teacher, therefore, has a strong need for a valid perspective on teaching, a clear concept of Scripture, and a workable knowledge of the Bible.

A Valid Perspective on Teaching

Communication. That's the word for teaching. Communicating the word of God is the essence of the work of the Sunday School teacher. And there is no greater work to be done!

But, isn't *teaching* the Bible a subordinate function to *preaching* the Bible? Not in the Old Testament, even though most of the teaching was done in the home. Neither is Bible *teaching* subordinate to Bible *preaching* in the New Testament. Admittedly, teaching seems to rank lower than preaching in the minds of some teachers as well as some preachers. However, such an attitude would be extremely difficult to justify from the Scriptures, either directly or by implication. Both teaching and preaching are essential to the gospel ministry, and the lack or the weakness of either one causes them both to be less effective in fulfilling God's total purpose.

Preaching *(kerygma)* is the proclamation of the gospel, primarily to the nonbeliever, so that he can come to faith in Jesus Christ.

Teaching *(didaskein)* is the explanation of the gospel, primarily to the believer, so that he can understand his faith and grow in Christian grace.

Both teaching and preaching have the same content—the Word of God—and together these two highly related and interrelated functions constitute "the ministry of the Word." Teaching and preaching are equally essential to the dissemination of the Word of God, to the discipling of Christians, and to the dynamism of the church.

Teaching and preaching both are required to reach that marvelous goal, "Till we all come in the unity of the faith, and of the knowledge of the Son of God, unto a perfect man, unto the measure of the stature of the fullness of Christ" (Eph. 4:13).

When the aging apostle encouraged Timothy to "teach these great truths to trustworthy men who will, in turn, pass them on to others" (2 Tim. 2:2, TLB), he was referring to the communication of divine truth through teaching. Paul had been trained in the teaching methods of the Greeks in the school of Tyrannus at Ephesus. He was by training and experience highly qualified to speak on the merits of Bible teaching.

Bible teaching in the Sunday School is far from being what it should be or could be. Yet, it is a unique approach to doing what is needed to communicate the great truths of the Bible to the masses.

The Sunday School is unique in its approach to teaching. Teaching is generally done by ordinary people, for ordinary people. It is a quite common approach to a most uncommon challenge. More than anything else in a church the Bible teaching program is a program "*of* the people, *by* the people, and *for* the people."

Sunday School teaching is unique in its purpose. It is not a quasi-college or seminary. It is intended to produce learners rather than scholars. It is intended to be practical rather than academic. It is intended to help people handle the questions about life rather than settle all the questions about the hereafter. It is intended to be comprehensive rather than exhaustive. It is intended to complement preaching, never to compete with it.

Undoubtedly it is true that Bible teaching is the first

step in God's plan for transforming persons. It is this fact that gives the Sunday School its importance, and the Sunday School teacher his significance.

A Clear Concept of the Scriptures

A Sunday School teacher needs a clear understanding of the meaning of the Scriptures. The word means sacred writings. When the word is used with the adjective *holy*—which means set apart, separate, different—it refers to the sacred writings contained in the Bible. The biblical material is considered holy because of its content, its purpose, and its author—the Holy Spirit. The word *Bible* is simply a transliteration of the Greek *biblos,* meaning "book." "The Holy Bible" is the title given to the sacred Scriptures which include only the Old Testament in Judaism, but in Christianity both the Old and the New Testaments.

Although the concept is too technical to consider adequately in a book such as this, there is a sense in which the terms *scripture (graphe)* and *Bible (biblos)* have a somewhat different meaning. The word *scripture* is most frequently used in connection with a specific passage from the Bible. However, the word carries a strong connotation of both religious history and theology. The matter of divine inspiration is also involved. The word *Bible* is most frequently used to describe the entire Word of God and has a connotation of divine revelation. Matters such as the text, languages, translations, and other authenticative considerations are involved.

These distinctions between scripture and Bible are interesting, and it is good to be aware of them. But they properly belong to the area of advanced biblical scholarship. The average Sunday School teacher needs to be assured that for all practical purposes the Scriptures and the Bible are essentially one and the same. Whatever the sacred writings are called, they *are* the Word of God. This they claim to be in hundreds of references. Also, the Scriptures *are* the revelations of God. In almost two thousand instances they make this claim.

The magnificence of the Scriptures is that day by day, hour by hour, they have the unique quality of being again and again the fresh Word of God. This uniqueness grows out of the fact that the Bible is the truth of God and is therefore eternal truth. The prophet Jeremiah seemed to sense this eternal aspect when he wrote: "The Lord's lovingkindness indeed never cease,/For His compassions never fail./They are new every morning;/Great is thy faithfulness" (Lam. 3:22-23, NASB).

Most church people know that the Old Testament speaks of God's work in history before the coming of Christ, and that the New Testament is concerned with Christ and the early beginnings of the church. Christians believe that the New Testament is the fulfillment of the Old Testament and that the Old Testament is incomplete without the New Testament.

The concept of a covenant relationship between God and his people runs like a scarlet thread throughout the entire Bible. For example, see Genesis 9:8-17; Genesis 17; Exodus 19:5-6; Exodus 20; 34 and Matthew 26:27-28.

The word *covenant* or "agreement" probably is a better English translation for the Hebrew word *berith* than the word *testament.* The Old Testament (or covenant) is a record of God's dealings with Israel on the basis of the Law. However, Israel violated the covenant often. Over and over, God in his mercy forgave and renewed the covenant. Eventually, because Israel continually failed to honor her covenant with God, the new covenant of grace was made with God's new people, the church. This new and better covenant was sealed with the blood of God's own Son. The New Testament as we know it today is the written record of God's relationship to men then, now, and in the future.

In reality, a clear concept of Scripture goes far beyond a recognition of the two major divisions as the "Old" and "New." It reflects a conviction that these designations represent the two basic themes of the Bible more than they refer to times or history.

A Working Knowledge of the Bible

I desire for every teacher a working knowledge of the Bible that includes appreciation for how it came to be, awareness of its eternal timeliness, and an understanding of its unity and diversity.

1. The Bible is a divine book that is human.

At first glance the statement that the Bible is a divine book that is human may seem to be contradictory, but is it? Peter said: "For the prophecy came not in old time by the will of man: but holy men of God spake as they were moved by the Holy Ghost" (2 Pet. 1:21).

The Bible is divine in that it is God's own revelation of himself to man. It is human in that man recorded what God revealed. God's self-revelation did not occur all at one time, or all in one way. There were stages of revelation, but each stage was a preparation for the full and final revelation which came in the person of Jesus Christ. The writer of Hebrews says it this way: "Long ago God spoke in many different ways to our fathers through the prophets . . . telling them little by little about his plans. But now in these days he has spoken to us through his Son to whom he has given everything, and through whom he made the world and everything there is" (Heb. 1:1-2, TLB).

The biblical revelation came through men who were inspired by the Holy Spirit. How they were inspired is not revealed in the Bible. Apart from any of man's several *theories* about inspiration (and their attendant concerns with "biblical criticism"), there is one abiding *fact* about inspiration. Namely, God gave himself *out* to man in the act of revelation, and he gave himself *in* to man in the act of inspiration. To put it another way, the emergence of revelation *from* God brought with it a corresponding emergence *from* man—a record of the divine communication.

Apparently the biblical writers were so influenced by the Spirit that their work was "God-breathed," yet they expressed those God-given truths through their own unique personality and in their own personal style of writing. Such is the marvelous nature of inspired revelation.

Because the Bible is an inspired revelation, it is also an authoritative revelation. It is authoritative in its message, in religion, in the church, in the lives of Christians, and in all things to which it speaks. The only alternative to accepting the authority of the Bible is to substitute the authority of man for that of God.

2. The Bible is an ancient book that is new.

The writing of the Bible occurred during a period of approximately 1600 years. The book of Job was written about 1500 B.C. (by Moses?), and the final writings by John were compiled about A.D. 90 or a few years later.

Not only is the Bible very old, but it reflects the cultures of ancient and complex civilizations which no longer exist. Bible people are largely strangers to the Western world. Their customs are hard to understand; their values are often confusing; their practices are sometimes bewildering;

their languages are extremely complex; and their thinking processes are more concrete than abstract.

There is a great gulf to be bridged between biblical concepts and modern understanding of these concepts. Yet the very uniqueness of this problem is a great strength of the Scriptures. This very difference between the then and now only amplifies the fact that the Bible deals with our continuing problems: life, death, relationships, inequalities, wickedness, truth, rewards, reality, the hereafter, and all of the other pressing concerns which we share.

In other words, all of the experiences and situations found in the Bible are as fresh as the morning news and as relevant as today's commentaries. In the Bible, God speaks totally to the totality of life. By inspiration and guideline, by standard and measure, by precept and example, by admonition and exhortation, the Bible is a living word from God freshly spoken to every man in every situation. In the Bible, God is daily and continually confronting man in his need. It is in the Bible that God's Son becomes the reality of realities. It is in the Bible that an ancient book becomes the newest and freshest communication that man can comprehend.

3. The Bible is a diverse book that is unified.

At first glance the Bible may seem to be only a collection of the writings of various men. Although some thirty-five different writers can be identified, it seems clear that there is only one source—God.

Within the sixty-six books of the Bible there are many types of literature. There is law, history, hymns, poetry, wisdom, preaching, Gospels, church history, personal and church letters, and at least one apocalyptic book.

In addition to the diversity in the kind of literature in the Bible, the structure itself is most unusual. The Bible is not a chronological story of religious events. It is not a summary of world history, because it is quite selective in its material that relates to history. The Bible is not even arranged on a time sequence. For example, the book of Job is considered the oldest book in the Old Testament, and Mark the oldest in the New Testament; yet neither book comes first in its division of the Bible.

The biblical structure also includes some material that is repeated in more than one place and in somewhat different form; yet there is an obvious integrity not only within the particular book but in the Bible as a whole. This integrity is possible because the Bible presents the same God all the way from Genesis to Revelation. He is Jehovah in the Old Testament, and the God and Father of our Lord Jesus Christ in the New Testament.

Just as there is only one God throughout the Bible, there is essentially only one theme running through the two Testaments. That theme is the redemption of man which is finally and fully realized in Jesus Christ. Without Christ there would be no redemption, and without Christ there would likely be no Bible. He is the central, unifying focus of all the Scriptures.

An Understanding of Biblical Interpretation

Because the Sunday School is really a Bible school, the teacher automatically finds himself in the role of a biblical interpreter. Being an interpreter means, among other things, that the teacher not only studies for himself but also for those whom he guides in Bible study. It puts upon the teacher a heavy dual responsibility: to guide learners in the discovery and meaning of genuine truth; and to avoid the pitfalls of misapplication, false conclusions, and dissemination of error.

In a real manner the first letter to Timothy is an appeal

from Paul for a diligent and responsible effort in teaching and interpreting the Holy Scriptures.

Timothy had observed Paul's life and had seen how Paul demonstrated his own teaching in his personal conduct. But imitating an example, even a superb example, is not enough. Like present-day Sunday School teachers, Timothy needed to know how to teach the truth and interpret it accurately. Paul's classic statement, "rightly dividing the word of truth" (2 Tim. 2:15), may be translated also as "skillfully teaching the word of truth." Perhaps *The Living Bible* paraphrase, "Know what His word says and means," states it most succinctly.

Interpretation of the Bible has always been an important and challenging task. It is rooted in Old Testament precedent, in New Testament practice, and in contemporary efforts to get a better understanding of the Bible. Unfortunately, for the untrained interpreter, the very thought is frightening and even faith-shaking at times. On the other hand, biblical interpretation has developed into both an art and a science. It is an exciting and rewarding experience to persons who understand its purposes, procedures, and tools.

In a nutshell, interpretation is the process of seeking to learn exactly what the writer had to say, to comprehend what the writer meant for his readers to conclude, and to help others gain an accurate understanding of the thought.

Although scholars are generally in agreement on most of the teachings of the Bible, there is still room for much improvement in both the theory and practice of interpretation, especially on the level of the lay teacher in the Sunday School.

To become a better interpreter a teacher needs to work constantly in some specific areas:

1. Getting a growing understanding of the Bible as a whole

2. Securing and using satisfactory versions and translations of the Bible

3. Developing an understanding of the background out of which the Scriptures emerged

4. Searching for the exact meaning of biblical words

5. Understanding and considering the form and style of biblical literature

6. Interpreting each passage in the light of the whole body of biblical truth

Many good books are available to help the teacher in his continuing search for understanding, but nothing is better than a serious and continuing reading of the Bible itself in as many translations as possible.

The teacher who takes seriously his matchless opportunity to guide other learners into a knowledge of the truth will be rewarded by seeing his members grow in understanding, faith, and Christian experience. He will rejoice in being able to glorify the heavenly Father by making his truth known and understood. Thus he will be doing something for his class members that even the angels in heaven are not privileged to do!

> Teach the Word, my teacher friend,
>   Teach the Word;
> For there's nothing more important
>   To be done.
> Angels from the realms of glory,
>   Cannot tell salvation's story;
> It requires those whom
>   God's grace has won!

> —JOHN T. SISEMORE

5
Make a Difference

The large sign by the roadside was sensational. Even to an experienced educator its message was surprising and startling. In only six short words it boldly affirmed what amounted to an educational philosophy, objective, and a means to achieve the objective. The sign read: "Make a difference—be a teacher."

Ah, yes! Make a difference. That is both the underlying philosophy and the main purpose in teaching. Making a difference is what *all* teaching is all about, and making a difference is the essence of the Sunday School teacher's task.

But what kind of difference should teaching make? A quantitative difference? A qualitative difference? The answer is unmistakable. Teach to make *more* persons *better* persons. That is the only kind of teaching that really makes a difference.

From the Christian vantage point the word *desirable* should be added to "difference." Teaching should make a *desirable difference*. The phrase *desirable difference* is a relative term and like all other relative terms, it requires a norm, a standard by which it can be measured. In Sunday School teaching the standard is what the Bible teaches about any given subject. Nothing else will suffice. Even statements of faith, creeds, or church-designed standards are not necessarily adequate.

If teaching makes a desirable difference, there is an inherent need for some way to determine the kind and amount of difference that is achieved. This need requires some form of evaluation, criteria, or testing.

In recent years, religious educators have developed a variety of approaches to appraising the outcomes of learning and the effectiveness of teaching. Many, if not most of these methods, have been borrowed or adapted from secular educators.

Although each type of evaluation is useful, there still seems to be something vital missing in all tests and evaluations when they are applied to Christian teaching and learning. In general, evaluations can test only mental, behavioral, and personality changes. Because persons can be conditioned to respond to a predetermined standard in these areas, the response may not be fully authentic. In addition, the spiritual dimensions of teaching and learning also need to come into the evaluation picture. The spiritual aspect introduces into evaluation an altogether different quality, because it is the integrating factor that ties intelligence, behavior, and personality into a wholeness of personhood.

It is obviously most difficult to evaluate spiritual matters such as the quality of one's Christian experience or the depth of one's Christian commitment. It may even be impossible to ascertain the degree of spiritual growth or the attainment of a personality that is genuinely Christian.

Even though it is difficult to evaluate the spiritual dimensions of learning, it is certain that both the teacher and class members will pass judgment on such matters. Sometimes they will be able to verbalize their evaluations effectively. Much of the time they will be aware of only a vague feeling of satisfaction or dissatisfaction with their spiritual progress. Nevertheless, they are evaluating their learning experiences, and this evaluation has far-reaching implications. Many Sunday School dropouts are simply demonstrating their feeling that they are not getting what they wanted or needed.

Surely there can be and should be a more effective means of determining the spiritual value of the learning experience. Because evaluation is simply the comparison of what *is* as opposed to what *ought* to be, there are only two factors involved in valid evaluation. First, there must be some commonly accepted objectives or standards (what *ought* to be) for the group. For a Sunday School, some of the standards of evaluation are: (1) an experience of conversion; (2) becoming a member of a church; (3) growing in biblical knowledge and understanding; (4) developing improved attitudes toward and appreciation for the Christian way of life; (5) improving standards and habits of conduct; and (6) increasing use of one's talents and skills in Christian service.

Second, if evaluation of the spiritual dimensions of learning is to be valid, there must be an understanding of where members are (what *is*) to use in measuring their progress toward the norm or standard (what *ought* to be).

There are several norms available, and the remainder of this chapter is concerned with these standards of measurement. As a starting point, it is well to remember that the ultimate test of all educational efforts is the *kind* of persons that emerge from the educational influence. In reality, the final test of Sunday School teaching is the *quality* of Christian men and women it produces.

In a more specific way, it must be kept in mind that the Christian life has a number of very exact and concrete demands. These demands are moral, ethical, and spiritual in nature. These demands, when met, are reflected in the personal daily life of the Christian. The presence of these qualities is a readily obvious indication of progress in Christian learning and also an accurate measure of the Sunday School teacher's achievement.

The qualities that make a difference between Christians and non-Christians may be stated in a variety of ways, but they will eventually include such things as the learner's faith, goals, values, integrity, commitments, relationships, personality, and life-style.

Stimulate Vital Faith

If you and I are to make a difference in the lives of our members, we must begin at the point of stimulating a vital faith. The Christian life begins with faith—faith in the reality of Jesus Christ. In some ways this is a simple faith, because it is a matter of belief. It accepts the factual testimony of history about Jesus Christ and the events surrounding his life, death, and resurrection. Belief agrees with the theological proposition of Paul that "Christ died for our sins" (1 Cor. 15:3). Belief acknowledges that God's Son not only saved man from his sin but also from the penalty of his sin.

In believing these foundational concepts of Christianity, an individual is exercising a kind of faith that is based largely on knowledge. This factual knowledge is essential, but it is only the beginning of faith. There is more, much more, to an authentic Christian faith. First, there is the unique way that a "believer" must *experience* faith. Unless there is an emotional response of love for Christ, implanted by the Holy Spirit, and accompanied by repentance for sin, an individual has accepted only a body of religious facts. He has not experienced a saving faith in Jesus Christ.

When a person experiences faith, he moves from knowing *what* he has believed to knowing *whom* he has believed. (See 2 Tim. 1:12.) The evidence of having a faith experience is for the person to make progress in loving God with all his heart and his neighbor with an emotion that is equivalent to the concern for himself.

There is no aspect of Sunday School teaching that needs or deserves more careful attention than the distinction between the *exposure* to the truth and an *experience* with the truth. There is no privilege that exceeds that of leading class members from exposure to experience.

Encourage Distinctive Commitment

The admonition that someone has given teachers is to "teach for a verdict." The verdict is commitment. The Christian life originates in a believing faith, but the deeper Christian experience grows out of a deeper quality of faith. This kind of faith is characterized by a distinctive commitment to Christ. It is a total commitment of the total person to the total control of Christ. Such a commitment is the difference between *beginning* the Christian life and *living* the life.

This kind of commitment involves the intellect, because it requires an unquestioning faith in God. It involves the emotions, because it requires an unbounded love for Christ. It involves the volitional powers, because it requires an unceasing surrender of the will to the Holy Spirit. These are the essential elements of total commitment.

Commitment of this quality and depth is undoubtedly the most pressing need of this, and any, generation of Christians. Nothing else will overcome the shallow, ineffective, and unproductive life of so many who are "keeping up the forms of religion but not giving expression to its power" (2 Tim. 3:5, Williams).

The ultimate purpose of Sunday School teaching is to bring persons to a thoroughly responsible commitment to the lordship of Christ and into a continuing discipleship with Christ. This may seem unnecessary, if not trite, but it will be impossible for a teacher to achieve this purpose if he has not made his own distinctive commitment and is not enjoying it as a personal experience. If this commitment has not been made, or if it needs to be freshened by a renewed affirmation, the words of this lovely song may be helpful:

"His Way—Mine"

God has a place for ev'ry planned creation
  A path for ev'ry star to go
He drew the course for ev'ry river's journey
  Now I know he has a way for me.
I place my life in the hands of God
  Those hands so scarred now outstretched for me.
Wherever it may be, over land, over sea
  May Thy will sublime, oh Thou God divine be
  mine.[1]

—Bo Baker

Lift Up Worthy Goals

The need for Bible teaching that lifts up worthy goals has never been more urgent. In contemporary life there is a strong emphasis on personal, family, corporate, church, and even spiritual goals. Granted that there is much to be said in favor of a goal-oriented life, family, business, and church. Yet there is also a genuine danger in this

---

[1] © Copyright 1955, Richard D. Baker. All rights reserved. Published by Richler, a division of Crescendo Music Publications, Inc. Used by permission.

concept. The danger is that a person—in pursuing his own goal-setting, strategy planning, and action-taking initiative—may overlook the fact that God already has a plan for him. To ignore this fact, or to fail to take it into account, is to exemplify presumption and probably arrogance.

Every person should have an integrating center around which he builds his life. Everyone needs to have something first in his life. Every individual needs to have at least a hope of eventual achievement. Whatever goals these needs may prompt become the supreme loyalty which determines everything else a person does in life and with his life. The ironic thing is that everyone has goals and serves them even when he is not aware that they exist.

For the Christian, a knowledge of God's plan for his life is the integrating center around which he should build. For the Christian, Jesus Christ must be the supreme loyalty of life. For the Christian, the Holy Spirit must be the prompting, energizing, and motivating power of one's life. When these divine realities are properly understood and appropriately internalized into the Christian's goals and ambitions, the world's standards of success are recognized as sinking sand, and the one who builds on them seems shallow, if not foolish.

Sunday School teaching is dramatically tested by the quality of the goals the learners adopt. When class members assure that their lives belong only to them, and that they are free to do with them as they please, they have either failed to learn or they have failed to have the right teaching.

The Bible does not condemn planning for one's life and its future realization. It does indicate that Christians need to strongly consider the uncertainty of the future and God's purpose for the future. The Williams translation of James

4:13-15 puts goals, planning, and ambition into the proper Christian perspective: "Come now, you who say, 'Today or tomorrow we are going to such and such a city and stay a year, go into business and make money,' although you do not have the slightest knowledge of tomorrow. What is the nature of your life? It is nothing but a mist which appears for a little while and then disappears. Instead, you ought to say, 'If the Lord is willing, we shall live and do this or that.' "

In the Christian life, all goals, plans, and dreams should be made in the context of God's leadership. Would you agree that directing teaching toward this outcome is vitally involved in the admonition to "make a difference"?

Guides Toward Christian Life-Style

The apostle Peter raised the most basic question possible with reference to the Christian pattern of life: "What sort of persons ought you to be"? (2 Pet. 3:11, RSV). A teacher needs to find a satisfactory answer to this question if he is to help members develop a Christian life-style.

Few if any subjects are treated more extensively in the New Testament than the uniqueness of the Christian style of living. To be sure there is not a formal statement of specific step-by-step Christian behavioral characteristics. But there are numerous qualities recorded which distinguish the Christian from the non-Christian. The pattern of Jesus is held up both as a goal and an example (John 13:15; 1 Pet. 2:21).

In essence the Christian life-style is a positive way of life. It is a life that glorifies Christ. It is a life-style that is the product of the Holy Spirit. Paul described this kind of life with such words as "love, joy, peace, patience, kindness, goodness, faithfulness, gentleness, and self-control" (Gal. 5:22-23, Williams).

The Christian life-style is also a disciplined manner of life. The desires and cravings of man's lower nature are the exact opposite of his new spiritual nature. The two natures constantly oppose each other. It is natural to be jealous, angry, and divisive; it requires constraint to be trusting, peaceful, and conciliatory. It is natural to engage in physical indulgences such as carousing, drinking, and drug abuse; it requires determination to avoid revelry, drunkenness, and debauchery.

The Christian life-style is a balanced way of life. This description does not refer to a balance between good and bad activities. It is rather a reference to the balance between what is believed and what is practiced. It is a balance between faith and works. It is a balance between Christian devotion and effective service to God. It is a balance between an intelligent response and an emotional response.

It is a balance between what *is,* as opposed to what *ought* to be. It is a balance between a wide range of Christian ministry and a high level of Christian witnessing. James, the beloved pastor of the church at Jerusalem, spoke poignantly to the matter of balance when he asked this question: "My brothers, what good is there in a man's saying that he has faith, if he has no good deeds to prove it?" (Jas. 2:14, Williams).

Create Awareness of the Potential for Wholesome Personality

Three basic facts, simple as they may seem, are essential to understanding what constitues a wholesome personality: (1) everyone has personality; (2) no two personalities are the same; (3) personality can be improved.

Personality is far more than the impression we make

on other people. Personality is the resultant quality which comes from the combination of all of a person's characteristics. It includes the physical structure, the style of behavior, the pattern of thinking, the manner of perception, and the tone of response. Because all persons possess these essential characteristics, all persons have personality. Even those persons who make no perceptible impression 'contribute nothing of themselves to others, and are distressingly bland, cannot be considered as having no personality. Even these persons emit a form of personality although it may seem "positively negative."

Although many people remind us of some other person, and are even quite similiar in some ways, no two persons have ever been completely alike, not even identical twins. Furthermore, people are constantly changing so that the same person is never really the same! This uniqueness in personality is termed *individuality*. Because individuality is an unmistakable facet of human personality, it cannot be ignored. This fact means that generalized statements about personality can be accurate only when they apply to those qualities that all persons have in common. For example: "All persons have personality. No two personalities are the same."

In teaching people, it is essential that the teacher thoroughly respect the divine provision of individuality. We blunder when we attempt to overly persuade or pressure our class members into becoming carbon copies of any other person—including ourselves. The only perfect pattern is Jesus Christ. Though we were designed to be like him, we recognize immediately that perfection is unattainable by mortal man. This fact holds even though man bears the image of God and possesses the component parts of the divine personality.

Every personality can be modified to a remarkable degree, even though certain boundaries are set by the circumstances of heredity. It is especially true that the person who becomes a Christian has a whole new potential for personality improvement.

In the new birth the Christian receives a new mind. The mind is not just made over—it is made anew. There is a new capacity for "wisdom, and righteousness, and sanctification, and redemption" (1 Cor. 1:30).

The Christian also has a new capacity for love. This faculty is not only an enlarged capability, it is also a completely new ability. It is the capacity to love God and to love one another as God loves us.

When a person becomes a Christian, he receives a new volitional power. It is the ability and the capacity to will to do the will of God. Undoubtedly the will is the hardest of all the personality components to change and improve. It is the essential cause of the disaster that overtook man in the fall. It is the last stronghold of the natural man against the spiritual man. When the Christian hands over his own will to God, he can have blessed fellowship between *his* mind and God's mind, *his* heart and God's heart, *his* will and God's will. And this experience is both the time and the way that Christian personality becomes wholesome, healthy, and pure.

In my opinion, teaching, even Bible teaching, is not primarily focused on changing and improving personality. If growth of the learner is the basic teaching goal, and it is, then personality improvement is primarily a concomitant of learning. If personality improvement occurs, it is a valid evidence that the learner is growing.

Can teaching make a desirable difference in persons without the teacher being caught up in an amateurish effort to modify personality? Indeed! The teacher may teach to help learners find a vital faith, to make a distinctive commitment to Christ, to work toward worthy goals, and to develop a Christian life-style. When some success is achieved in these efforts, personality is modified "here a little, there a little" until the man of God is "adequate, equipped for every good work" (2 Tim. 3:17, NASB). Then the teacher may be assured that his teaching has *really* made a difference.

This poem by Clarence Edwin Flynn summarizes some of the significant ways in which a teacher makes a difference.

"The Teacher"

He is a lighter of torches.
He is a lifter of skies,
A pusher-out of horizons
For eager, adventurous eyes.
He is a planter of gardens,
That beauty may grow by the door.
He is a merchant of wisdom
With never-diminishing store.

He is a builder of courage.
He is a tracer of ways.
He is a shaper of futures.
He is a molder of days.
He is a keeper of values.
He is a guide in the night.
He is a questor of wonder.
He is a man with a light.

6
Find Your Strength

"God has given each of us the ability to do certain things well. . . . If you are a teacher, do a good job of teaching" (Rom. 12:6-7, TLB).

Have you ever asked yourself: How in the world did I get into this teaching business? Or have you ever looked with an envious eye at a more experienced teacher and wondered, perhaps aloud, Why can't I be just half as good a teacher as he is? Likely you have even looked at yourself in a mirror and recognized the signs of discouragement and frustration, and sickness of heart enveloped you because your teaching was on dead center.

Some of these same emotions had piled up on the disciples when they realized that Christ's departure was imminent (John 14). They were thoroughly discouraged and frustrated. They were ashamed of their selfishness and pride. They were distressed because one of their own number was going to betray the Lord.

Their whole world seemed ready to collapse, and their minds were filled with haunting questions: "We haven't any idea where you are going, so how can we know the way?" (John 14:5, TLB). "Show us the Father and we will be satisfied" (John 14:8, TLB). "Why are you going to reveal yourself only to us disciples and not to the world?" (John 14:22, TLB).

All Sunday School teachers need to hear those reassuring

words of the Master Teacher: "Let not your heart be troubled" (John 14:1). "I will pray the Father, and he shall give you another Comforter" (John 14:16).

Even the very best Sunday School teachers will sometimes experience discouragement. But a frantic and feverish frustration ought not to be a part of the teacher's experience. These feelings are the inevitable result of human effort unaided by the power of the Holy Spirit.

God not only expects a type of Christian service that is characterized by assurance, poise, and equanimity but he has also provided for it. This kind of service is that which is done when we have found our strength and enablement in the Holy Spirit. Paul's admonition, "Find your strength in the Lord" (Eph. 6:11, NEB), implies an unlimited reservoir of support and assistance. A further implication is that strength from the Lord is specifically directed toward any given area of human need or weakness.

Finding your strength as a teacher waits on knowing, understanding, accepting, and relying on some precious truths about the teacher and his relationship to the Holy Spirit.

You Have a Gift

Remember that God through his generous grace has given gifts to all persons. Some of these gifts are natural because they come through the process of physical birth. Generally these gifts are in the form of a capacity. They are latent talents which become abilities or skills only through the process of disciplined effort. These are general gifts of God which are distributed only as God chooses.

There are also special spiritual gifts from God. They are spiritual because they are received as a result of an individual's spiritual rebirth. Admittedly, it is difficult to know if these gifts were given *with* the new birth, *after* the new birth, or if they are given as part of the process of growing in Christian maturity. Perhaps all three concepts are valid.

As a Christian, and especially as a teacher, you have both natural and spiritual talents. The Bible refers to all of these gifts as *charismata*, that is, gifts of God's Spirit. These gifts are given to every Christian, and they cover a wide variety of specialties.

If the frequency of reference to teaching in the Bible is significant, it is logical to believe that Bible teaching is the most widely distributed and most often needed of all spiritual gifts. It could hardly be coincidental that all three of the outstanding Bible characters—Moses, Christ, and Paul—were deeply concerned with the teaching of the Holy Scriptures. Paul had a deep conviction that teaching was a gift of God to be used in helping others learn about God. He expressed his conviction: "Some of us have been given special ability . . . caring for God's people . . . leading and teaching them in the ways of God" (Eph. 4:11, TLB).

As a Sunday School teacher you were selected and elected by your church. This is an honor because others have discerned that God has endowed you with a special ability. However, as a Christian teacher you were first elected, endowed, called, and empowered to perform your spiritual ministry of "caring . . . leading . . . teaching" by God himself.

As a God-called and empowered Sunday School teacher, you are not doing your own thing, or even the church's thing. You are first and foremost doing God's thing—that is, caring . . . leading . . . teaching. And the ability to do God's thing is his unmerited grace gift deposited in your life, to be used in his service, in the power of his Spirit. The purpose of the gift is the equipping of the believers to be ministers (not all ministers are pastors).

Peter wrote: "As each has received a gift, employ it for one another, as good stewards of God's varied grace . . . as one who renders it by the strength which God supplies; in order that in everything God may be glorified through Jesus Christ" (1 Pet. 4:10-11, RSV).

It seems inescapable that each Christian is held accountable for his gift(s) of the Spirit. These gifts are to be faithfully used for the common good of the church. To misuse or fail to use your gift of teaching is to prostitute that part of God himself which he has entrusted to your stewardship. What an awesome responsibility is involved in God's gift of teaching. And what a magnificent privilege is involved in having received this special ability. It is God's personal investment in you. It is your gift!

You Have a Teacher

Because Jesus was preeminently a teacher, it is not surprising that he presented the Holy Spirit as a teacher. In speaking to his disciples (learners) he said: "If you love me, obey me; and I will ask the Father and he will give you another Comforter, and he will never leave you. He is the Holy Spirit, the Spirit who leads you into all truth" (John 14:15-16, TLB). "But when the Father sends the Comforter instead of me—and by the Comforter I mean Holy Spirit—he will teach you much, as well as remind you of everything I myself have told you" (v. 26, TLB).

The "visible" teacher, you, have an invisible Teacher—the Holy Spirit. He is a teacher that "leads you into all truth." He is the Teacher who "will teach you much." He is the Teacher who will remind you of everything that Jesus taught. These statements about the teaching ministry of the Holy Spirit lead to four basic conclusions:

1. *Teaching* the truth of God's Word cannot be done successfully without the assistance of the Holy Spirit.
2. *Learning* the truth of God's Word cannot be done effectively without the teaching support of the Holy Spirit.
3. *Understanding* the truth of God's Word correctly cannot be possible without the special aid of the Holy Spirit.
4. *Remembering* the truth of God's Word accurately is dependent on the support of the Holy Spirit.

Notice how closely intertwined are these elements of education—teaching, learning, understanding, remembering—with the explicit work of the Holy Spirit. Undoubtedly the Holy Spirit is the teacher's Teacher. If this is not the case, or if the teacher chooses to depend on his own intelligence, his own skill, his own personality, and his own forcefulness, there is no dynamic in teaching. And there is no satisfactory outcome in learning.

There is a unique interrelationship between the teacher's *endowment* and the Spirit's *enduement*. It is possible for a Sunday School teacher to view the Spirit as just an accessory, a power supply, with all of the credit for success in teaching accruing to the teacher. In this case the Spirit is relegated to a place of mere endowment. On the other hand, the teacher may view the Spirit as the chief Teacher, and himself as a co-teacher who lends himself to the Holy Spirit. In this case, the Spirit provides enduement. Until a teacher sees himself as the instrument of the Spirit through which God communicates the word of truth, a teacher may be as much a hindrance to learning as he is potentially a help to learning.

You Have an Enabler

In John 14:16 Jesus told his disciples: "I will pray the Father, and he shall give you another Comforter, that he may abide with you for ever." The Greek word for Comforter is *parakletos*. It may also be translated as counselor, helper, and guide. The literal meaning is "called alongside." The Holy Spirit is at one and the same time both *inside* and *alongside* the teacher. There is no position or place that is not adequately covered by the Spirit's presence.

John's use of the word for "another" Comforter does not mean another kind *(heteros)* but another of the same kind *(allos)*. The Spirit is the *same* kind of teacher, helper, guide, and inspirer as Jesus was to his disciples. In the most real way possible, the *parakletos* is actually Jesus himself in his invisible, continuing presence. And he is doing substantially for us the same things he did for his disciples.

The Greek word *parakletos* is extremely difficult to translate adequately. The Greek word sums up all of the many functions of the Holy Spirit, but there is no English word that adequately communicates these functions. In the final analysis, it is impossible to adequately define the Holy Spirit because he is the ever-present reality of God. Furthermore, is it hopeless to try listing all of the roles he fills, or to delineate all of the functions he performs. The Holy Spirit defies description!

From the perspective of the Sunday School teacher, the word *enabler* is probably as good a word as we can find to describe the Holy Spirit in his role of helping the teacher. The word *enable* means to authorize, endow, invest with power.

The Holy Spirit enables the teacher to understand the truth. Jesus said, "When he, the Spirit of truth, is come, he shall guide you into all the truth" (John 16:13, ASV). Because God is the source of all truth, there is but one Spirit of truth. Therefore, wherever and whenever truth is found, it is God's truth. And it is God's Spirit that enables the learner to find and understand that truth. Despite what some pseudo philosophers say, there is an ultimate and absolute truth because truth originates in God, and it is revealed by the Spirit of truth.

On the day of Pentecost the Spirit enabled teachers to both understand and communicate truth so people from all nations and languages could understand the truth of the gospel. In some ways at least, Pentecost was a reversal of the confusion at the Tower of Babel (see Gen. 11:1-9). At Babel, communication was disrupted by the confusion of languages. At Pentecost the Spirit restored the ability to communicate by giving men the instant ability to use *other languages* to explain the truth of God. The Christian communicator, by whatever name he may be called, is the Spirit's instrument in revealing, understanding, and communicating God's truth.

Just as the *Spirit* of God glorifies the *Son* of God through the written *Word* of God, he also breathes life into the printed page. Therefore, the teacher is not only enabled to discover truth, but he also has the truth revealed to him by the same Holy Spirit who inspired its preparation.

There is a glorious plus factor for the teacher who accepts the Spirit's revelation of, and guidance into, truth. The plus is a gradual progression "into *all* truth" (John 16:13).

The limitations of a finite mind and the disadvantage of inaccurate or incomplete insight may keep a teacher from a complete realization of "all truth." However, the Spirit will reveal all that the teacher needs and will use at any given time.

The Enabler guides the teacher in the teaching of Bible truth. What the Holy Spirit does *for* the teacher, he will also do *through* the teacher. Namely, he will act as the learner's Guide "into all truth," and he does this much in the same way Jesus taught his disciples.

On numerous occasions the Bible reveals how the disciples were perplexed at some of Jesus' teachings. Afterward, they asked him privately for further instruction. At least as great a privilege is available to the Sunday School teacher. He may ask the Spirit for further instruction, and he may also ask for help in causing the class members to understand Bible truth.

The Spirit is preeminently qualified for this assistance. He is the source of the Bible. If anyone understands the Bible, and if anyone can help others understand it, he can. Paul expressed this concept: "No one can really know what anyone else is thinking, or what he is really like, except that person himself. And no one can know God's thoughts except God's own Spirit. And God has actually given us his Spirit . . . to tell us about the wonderful free gifts of grace and blessing that God has given us" (1 Cor. 2:11-13, TLB).

To study the Bible under the guidance of the Spirit is a cherished privilege. But to teach the Bible under the direct enablement of the Spirit is an incomparably greater privilege. It would be a tragedy for a teacher to try to carry the burden of teaching alone when the Holy Spirit is right beside him, and inside him, just waiting to be allowed to help. This enablement in teaching is what God's Spirit was given to provide. When the teacher allows the Spirit to help, he has teaching power. Otherwise, he is merely going through the motions and suffering the agony of obvious failure. It is God's Spirit who provides the necessary wisdom and the indispensable power required in the successful teaching-learning experience.

The Enabler aids the teacher in producing learning outcomes. The basic purpose in teaching is to stimulate desirable change in the life of the learner. This purpose has within it the possibility of manipulation and is therefore potentially capable of abuse. Every teacher must constantly maintain a healthy respect for the learner and keep his best interest at heart. He must remember that the learner is made in the image of God and so it is God's prerogative to determine and bring about the change within the learner.

An accurate translation of John 16:8 would read: "When he is come, he will *persuade* the world." It is obvious that the Holy Spirit does not coerce persons, even into learning the truth. If God's Spirit does not coerce, God's teachers should also refrain from pressure, compulsion, or undue insistence.

The teacher's role in producing learning outcomes should be confined to supportive activities such as informing, interpreting, applying, conferring, and advising. It is the work of the Spirit to convict, urge, and persuade. And it is the sole prerogative of the learner to make the decision to change, adjust, alter, modify, and develop. It is quite likely that most Sunday School teachers would be more serene, and probably more effective, if they would remember that the Holy Spirit honors the dignity of a person and is willing to let the individual make his own decisions.

Teaching for results is quite in harmony with the concept

of Christian teaching, but *pressuring* for results violates the dignity of the learner and usurps the persuading role of the Holy Spirit.

There is a quiet, unseen, ever-present Friend, Partner, and unfailing Source of Strength upon whom the Sunday School teacher may rely. He is the supreme Reality in the life of the Christian teacher. He stands ready to be the supreme Power in the work of the teacher. He is able and ready to turn ineffectiveness into effectiveness, and failure into success. It is in him that the teacher finds his help, support, and strength. So rejoice, teacher friend. Incomparable resources are yours in the Holy Spirit!

7
Serendipities

It was only a few moments before a Sunday School conference was to begin when an usher gave me a note. It was an urgent appeal to call a number at once. When I placed the call, an excited voice identified a dear friend from years gone by. The lady was too old to still be alive (I thought)! In answer to my cautious question she said, "I am ninety years old now, but I still teach my class every Sunday."

This lady had been teaching for seventy years. Surely she was worn out with all of the responsibilities related to an adult Sunday School class. I asked another question: "Why do you still teach at this advanced age?" The quick response was thrilling. "It is the greatest joy of my life. I work hard at keeping fresh in my teaching, and the Lord gives me new joys that I never imagined I'd have." There it is. Serendipity!

The real answer to success in any endeavor is the joy that comes from diligent effort. But isn't it impossible to work faithfully at doing something well without experiencing a large measure of personal satisfaction and joy? Aren't there those unexpected expressions of divine favor? Is there any reason why teaching a Sunday School class would be an exception to this wonderful overflow of God's goodness?

There are few, if any, experiences that give a greater dimension of satisfaction, reward, and pure delight than those unplanned, unexpected, and unpredictable blessings connected with the work of a Sunday School teacher. It *is* all joy, even the hard work, if you can sense these serendipities of the Spirit.

Serendipity: Lesson Preparation

Although lesson preparation, like any other kind of intellectual effort, can be tiring, it doesn't have to be boring or dull. One of the chief rewards in preparation is the mental stimulation and sense of achievement which it provides. There is a certain exultation that comes from feeling that you can anticipate what is likely to happen on Sunday morning.

Another joy found in lesson preparation is that of escaping the superficial, "once-over-lightly" routine on Saturday evening. Preparation that is habitually this haphazard reveals a character flaw. It is always weakness, if not immaturity, to live on a day-to-day, or even on a Sunday-to-Sunday basis. A periodic, planned study schedule that provides for continuity and concentration of effort is essential. Concentration on the matter at hand is a mark of strength and a characteristic of the mature person. It is generally the main difference between success and failure in any enterprise.

Because concentration is a mental process, it can be learned. It begins with a decision, an act of the will, an imposition of the self-discipline required to make proper preparation for the teaching experience. Deliberate concentration and disciplined study present one of the choicest pleasures in teaching. It is the anticipation of the outcome before the actual act of teaching occurs.

The joy of preliving the experience of teaching takes place in those long, and sometimes tiring, hours of study, planning, and organizing. This unique joy occurs because the prepared teacher senses that he will not be teaching the "same old stuff." He knows that preparation has enriched his own knowledge and understanding—that his teaching will be alive and dynamic—that he can avoid the anguish of running dry and escape the frustration of teaching too near the edge of his preparation.

There is another joy arising out of the experience of preparation. It is the stimulation that comes from reading and studying the sources of information related to the lesson taught. As I write this chapter, I have thirty-seven different sources before me. I have researched each one of them without any real success in finding useful ideas. Yet there is an indescribable delight that comes from reading, searching, thinking, considering, judging, analyzing, accepting, rejecting, and formulating ideas. Preparation is a priceless jewel which delivers tremendous satisfaction to its owner.

Serendipity: Human Involvement

It is a rather well-known fact that class members do not necessarily learn the most from the teacher who *knows* the most. Actually they learn the most from the teacher with whom they *associate* the most. Whatever else may be said about teaching and learning, it must be said that both processes are greatly influenced by the quantity and quality of the interpersonal relationships between the teacher and the learner. Human involvement is in itself a remarkable teaching-learning experience.

Apparently Jesus had a strong commitment to personal involvement with his learners. His disciples not only learned from him—they lived with him throughout his ministry. How can we possibly determine the full value

of this most personal involvement in the life of his learners? Undoubtedly they heard his messages, listened to his parables, pondered over his words of wisdom, and observed his remarkable miracles. But did these things, as important as they were and are, mean as much to their learning as his involvement in their day-to-day relationships?

Not only the best, but the most lasting aspects, of teaching are those impressions which the teacher deposits in the life of his members. These impressions may be planned, incidental, or even accidental—nevertheless they are real and significant parts of teaching.

In the area of human development the minister and the Sunday School teacher have essentially the same opportunity. The main difference is in the number of persons they serve. Their constituents look upon them not only as friends and fellow Christians but also as intimate personal guides through life's experiences. These persons expect more than the normal experiences of the Sunday School and church. When special needs arise, when trouble comes, when a crisis hits, the reality of the teacher-member relationship is tested. If there is no guidance given, no consolation offered, no effort to help meet the need, there is obviously only a superficial relationship. It is at this point that the person in need is doubly hurt by the realization that the teacher doesn't really care.

Becoming involved in the acute personal needs of the members is the essence of being a Christian teacher. Ministering to human distress is not only being like Christ—it is Christ ministering through the teacher.

In some cases a teacher may not be able to offer much real assistance. However, he can at least visit the member in need. Company is supporting. Being present when a need arises is expressing sympathy, concern, and even love.

Consolation can be given just in the act of standing by. Probably everything that is said will be forgotten or only partially remembered, but the fact that the teacher made an effort and took the time to become involved will be remembered forever.

Times of need not only give the caring teacher an opportunity to minister in Jesus' name but they also offer splendid opportunities to do some excellent wayside teaching. Obviously this type of teaching refers to a person-to-person approach. It is that word of sympathy, the effort to explain, the bit of advice, the offering of a possible solution, the moment of prayer, or even the falling tear that communicates the reality of Christian love and compassion.

Although the task of the teacher is generally interpreted to mean the work that is done in the classroom, the best teaching may be done outside the classroom as the teacher becomes appropriately involved in the personal needs of the class members.

Serendipity: Leader Relationships

Just as Peter, James, and John formed the inner circle of the apostles, the Sunday School teacher is an important part of the inner circle of the church. Whether or not there should be an inner circle may be debatable. The fact that there always *is* an inner circle is hard to deny. This circle of relationships is not planned. It is caused. It is the inevitable result of people giving themselves to a common commitment, a common set of values, and a common set of loyalties.

In a church the most significant inner circle is almost always composed of the Sunday School leaders, particularly the teachers. The reason is quite apparent. The Sunday School leaders comprise the largest group of the most committed people in the church. The Sunday School staff is the church's largest number of people who believe in, and are committed to the values of Bible study, outreach, witnessing, ministry, and total church progress. Because they hold these things in common, they become united in mind, heart, spirit, and desire. These factors are the ingredients of real togetherness and Christian fellowship. The result is an inner circle just like that of which it is said, "They were all with one accord in one place" (Acts 2:1).

The Sunday School inner circle is rarely ever a power structure, but it does have a considerable measure of influence in the life of the church. This influence is neither unwholesome nor undesirable. The working force in any enterprise is both the reflection and the strength of the enterprise. Influence is also the most noticeable characteristic or image which the group projects.

To persons who work in the Sunday School there is a certain indescribable sense of pleasure and satisfaction that comes from being caught up in the inner workings of the Sunday School. Planning is one of those inner workings that stimulates joy. Although planning is hard work, there is a rewarding sense of achievement when the group contemplates what the reality of the plan promises. Bearing responsibility often rests heavily on the spiritual shoulders, but there is an unexpected pleasure that is born in the pain of accountability. The inevitable feeling of discouragement and frustration when effort seems fruitless can also turn into the sweetest joy and satisfaction when the tide turns even slightly toward success.

Unfortunately, those persons who never participate in the work of planning, who never bear any of the load of responsibility, and who never expend any personal effort on behalf of others, can rarely experience the excitement of peer relationships which belong to leaders. There is indeed a unique joy experienced by persons who participate in a leadership team. It is both a personal joy and a vicarious joy.

Serendipity: Being Taught

It is an unwarranted, if not ridiculous, assumption to think that simply because a person has been selected to teach a Sunday School class that he knows everything and that the class members know nothing. Pretense at this point is a fatal flaw because the "know-it-all" teacher is an obstacle to persons who want to learn. A teacher is not a fountain of wisdom to which the members, as empty pitchers, come to be filled.

Certainly a teacher may, and even should, know more than the members. He should be more experienced, more mature, wiser, more responsible, more judicious, and more skilled as a learner. Nevertheless, the teacher should avoid the faintest feeling that he is an authority, even if he is!

The teacher who truly guides learners in the discovery of truth will also learn many new things along the way. And more often than not, he will actually learn them from his own members, the very people he is seeking to teach!

For example, the teacher can learn what other adults think. Most teachers are at least a few years older than their members. Those few years can make a lot of difference in the way people think. Individuals are not only products of their culture but of the time in which their culture was formulating their mind-set, standards, values, attitudes, and motives.

If the members are even slightly younger than the teacher, the teacher must make an effort to understand some of the basic and significant differences between teacher and members. Some teachers may have difficulty with the openness, frankness, and unconventional standards of some younger adults. At the same time, the young adult may have a real problem with the pat answers, empty traditions, and inconsistent practices of many older adults. This kind of situation will require some *real* learning on the part of both teacher and members, but the teacher must take the lead. Why? The members are in varying stages of development and in many cases are still babes in Christ; some may not be Christians.

Even when the teacher and class members are of the same relative age level, there are still many differences in thinking that must be understood. There may be differing theological concepts, sociological attitudes, political persuasions, emotional triggers, intellectual levels, and social practices that must be handled in the true learning experience. Of course, if the teacher is able to "zip the lip" of every class member so that differences are not revealed, the problems will not surface. In such a case, though, teaching and learning may, for all practical purposes, cease.

Teachers can also learn how to employ their members in teaching. This suggestion in no way implies passing around the responsibility for a given lesson. It means that often one class member can say something to another class member that communicates better than what the teacher could say. Members will often accept from another member a corrective, even critical comment that would never be accepted from the teacher. Sometimes a member may express an untenable viewpoint, or sanction some course of action that is unchristian. If the teacher takes an opposite viewpoint, he appears to be authoritarian. Yet in the same situation another member could respond appropriately and acceptably.

Within every group of learners there is both group reinforcement and group correctiveness. These factors are very strong educative influences within the group. Wise indeed is the teacher who recognizes these forces and uses them appropriately in the teaching-learning experience. In this way the teacher not only shares in the joy of learning with the group but actually draws upon the resources of the group. In addition he receives the support and reinforcement which the group alone can produce.

Serendipity: Joyful Anticipation

"I can hardly sleep on Saturday nights," said a happy teacher, "because the anticipation of what may happen in my class on Sunday is so exciting."

Ah, yes, the excitement of anticipation. Teachers who have experienced it understand it thoroughly, but the ones who have not are even frustrated at the thought.

What makes anticipation so exciting? Is it the fellowship with the members? Is it the joy of helping others in their quest for Bible truth? Is it the overflow of spiritual enrichment that comes from studying, planning, and praying for the class session?

Yes, all of these produce much of the joy of anticipation that a teacher experiences. However, there is more. There is the *personal growth* that a teacher senses is occurring in his or her own life. This growth is wonderfully satisfying; it is cause for gratefulness to God. It is also an assurance that the teacher is not content with past achievements and is not on the road to "has-been-land." The real joy and excitement of what a teacher anticipates grows largely out of what he feels *may* happen, not what *has* happened, or even what *is* happening.

I have touched on only a few of the many day-by-day joys of teaching. Yet, they are enough to verify the proposition that teaching is a real joy, especially when you consider all of those unexpected blessings arising out of the routine aspects of teaching. These blessings are your spiritual serendipities.

As I was completing this chapter, a letter arrived bearing a rural route and box number. It was with trembling hand that the writer of the letter described herself as "your humble servant in Jesus Christ who has been teaching for fifty-seven years." The letter was a testimony of God's blessing and leadership through a long lifetime of teaching. Its closing sentence kindled a warm glow of delight in my own heart: *"It has been joy all the way."*

Serendipity!

8
Joy Unlimited

There he was in jail writing a letter to encourage his friends back at the church. In reality the church should have been trying to comfort him. After all, a prison isn't the best place in the world in which to be cheerful. But this was not a new experience for this man. He frequently gave encouragement when he himself could well have been the receiver of comfort and cheer. And he was in jail for doing something good rather than something bad. How easy it would have been to feel sorry for himself.

Here is what he was writing to his friends: "May God bless you all. Yes, I pray that God our Father and the Lord Jesus Christ will give each of you his fullest blessings, and his peace in your hearts and your lives. All my prayers for you are full of praise to God! When I pray for you, my heart is full of joy" (Phil. 1:2-4, TLB).

This kind of joy was not only a reflection of a deep inner security; it was also an elation that came as a result of his labors of love. Even in prison Paul was certain that his own unwelcome circumstances had turned out to be a greater progress of the gospel. Paul's attitude was not some superficial expression of positive thinking; it was a confident optimism that came from knowing that Christ would be honored whether he personally lived or died. This attitude gave him great joy, a joy springing from a lifetime of complete commitment, devoted discipline, and endless effort. It was joy unlimited.

Joy is not just an emotion of the moment. It is a mind-set, and the mind-set of the Sunday School teacher is both a cause and an effect. Joy comes from the teacher's enthusiasm for Bible teaching, his love for the learners, the pleasure of his work, and certainly the stimulation from his preparation for teaching. On the other hand, the effort expended in learning to love teaching, appreciate the members, undergo the hard work, and delight in the endless hours of study, is what produces the joy in the first place. So the effort produces the joy, and joy creates the mind-set.

In the role of a teacher, the Christian can experience what Paul enjoined: "Rejoice in the Lord always: and again I say, Rejoice" (Phil. 4:4).

Rejoice in Prospects Becoming Members

The most common image a teacher has of himself is the dispenser of answers to the questions of the members. This is a common error of almost all persons who are authorities in any field. Actually, the Sunday School teacher plays a unique preeducation role. He is first, at least chronologically, as much a finder, cultivator, and enlister of prospects as he is an educator. Only a casual review of the early ministry of Jesus will affirm that he gave himself continually to the ministry of outreach. Many teachers overlook this fact; some even hold the concept in contempt.

After writing an article in which I made an appeal for adult teachers to be diligent in the visitation of prospects, I received a thoroughgoing denunciation from an adult teacher who climaxed her criticism with the statement: "All you would do would be to turn teachers into cheap door-to-door salespeople. I wouldn't bemean myself with such idiotic activity." Maybe not, but Jesus did! And so did the early Christians. To fail to work at the enlistment of prospects is to miss one of the supreme joys in teaching.

George was my most devastating prospect. He not only resisted every effort to see him; he even refused to converse when I found him. After several unproductive visits he finally said: "Don't bother me anymore. I'm not coming to your class, and I don't want to see you around here again." He communicated, and I reciprocated!

Several months afterward, late on a summer Saturday, the urgency of trying to see George once more became unbearable. With plenty of reluctance and much uneasiness I approached him. He fell in my arms and cried out: "I thought you'd never come back." In a defensive maneuver I replied, "You told me not to come back." His answer still haunts me: "Yes, but I thought you knew I didn't mean it." On Sunday, George not only joined the class, but he was saved, and he joined the church as well. Seeing prospects become members—joy unlimited!

Certainly all prospects do not become members, and all visits do not produce immediate results. Nevertheless there is a thrilling reward in the effort. Isn't it really true that we visit a lot of people we never get, but we get a lot of people we never visit? But we wouldn't get a lot of people we never visit if we didn't visit a lot of people we never get. In God's harvest there are many joyful surprises.

Reaching people for Bible study is the foundational function of the Sunday School. As the leader of the class, the teacher has both by position and assignment the ultimate responsibility for reaching every person who could be considered a prospect.

Obviously the task of reaching people is much greater than the work of enrolling people. A prospect may never be enrolled, but he can be reached through cultivative visitation and conversational teaching. These continuing efforts place the emphasis appropriately on persons, and they give significance and meaning to organization, buildings, equipment, methods, and even curriculum. These are all means to an end—the reaching of people.

Every Sunday School teacher has several important functions to fulfill. However, all of them, including the teaching function, are significantly affected by the teacher's concept of outreach. The teacher needs to view outreach as an *idea* originating in the heart of God. He must see outreach as the central *theme* of the Bible. He should perceive outreach as the *purpose* which called Jesus to earth. He should look upon outreach as the *heartthrob* of Christianity. He should view outreach as the *evidence* of one's commitment to Christ. He should visualize outreach as the *expression* of genuine compassion. He should regard outreach as the ultimate *response* to a ready world.

When a teacher comes to understand and actually accepts the fact that working at reaching people is following precisely in the footsteps of Jesus, then he cannot escape an extraordinary sense of joy when one of his prospects finally becomes a member.

Rejoice in Members Becoming Learners

Probably the three most persistent concepts regarding the teaching-learning experience are (1) learning is mastering factual knowledge; (2) teaching is telling people the facts; and (3) hearing the facts is synonymous with understanding and accepting the facts. All three of these commonly accepted viewpoints are at least partially erroneous.

Learning is not knowing—it is *growing*. Teaching is not telling—it is *guiding*. Understanding is not hearing—it is *experiencing*.

The ultimate purpose in teaching is not to stuff the learner's mind full of abstract information, even biblical data, but to help the learner experience living with the truth until it becomes incarnate in his personality and character. Truth then, especially Bible truth, is much more than subject matter. Truth is an enabling power. It acts as a transforming catalyst. It results in a quality of being. Jesus said, "Ye shall know the truth, and the truth shall make you free" (John 8:32). The word *know (ginōskō)* not only means an intellectual concept but also an appreciation growing out of the relationship between the person knowing and the object known. Truth must, therefore, eventually become embodied in persons. Persons become the expression of truth!

It is a law of life that things do not remain the same. They either grow or they deteriorate. So, the Christian life cannot remain static or on a plateau. There must be growth, or there will be retrenchment. Growth is not only the result of learning; it *is* learning. So, teaching that causes learning also produces growth.

Growth (the result of learning) always involves change, many kinds of change. The mind is changed, ideas are changed, attitudes are changed, choices are changed, conduct is changed, the will is changed, emotions are changed, personality is changed, character is changed.

It is at the point of change that growth is observed. It is at the point of growth that learning is successful. It is at the point of learning that teaching is achieved. It is at the point of teaching that guidance is required.

It is a heavy responsibility to help learners understand

God's truth and redirect their lives in keeping with their understanding. Just as the disciples needed the help of Jesus in order to know, understand, and grow, so the members of every class need the same kind of guidance.

Providing this guidance is your blessed privilege as a teacher. Seeing changed lives as members become learners is one of the biggest causes for genuine rejoicing.

Rejoice in Learners Becoming Disciples

Christian learning never reaches its highest possibilities without resulting in discipleship. But discipleship is not some newly discovered doctrine with exotic spiritual overtones. It is an ancient concept. Socrates, the masterful teacher of the Greeks, popularized the concept "know thyself." Since, and before then, countless numbers of persons have been driven by the desire for self-knowledge. The popular identity question of today, "Who am I?" is just a modern phraseology of that same question.

Discipleship may be defined in several ways, but the word refers primarily to the state of being a copy or reproduction of a teacher and his way of life. The origin of the term is enlightening.

The English word *disciple* comes from the Latin word *discere* (to learn). The Greek word for disciple *(mathētēs)* means a learner. But in the Greek, the idea includes much more than being a pupil. The word is a compound (made up of two words or more) and means to work at following what has been learned. A disciple, therefore, is one who not only knows, but one who is a follower, an adherent, a facsimile, a personification of the one from whom he learned.

The first disciples of Jesus Christ were a very diverse group of persons. They were uniquely different from each other in their heritage, ability, temperament, and training. Some were quite gifted and capable persons, but most of them would be classified as ordinary common folk. Yet, they had some highly important characteristics that were unique to them and which give special meaning to the concept of being a disciple.

The original disciples were responsive to Christ's message and his call. They were loyal to him all their lives. But they made the same human errors that are common to all. Some of them made some extremely serious mistakes. Sometimes they allowed their emotions and ambitions to get the best of them. Even the best of the disciples sinned and failed Jesus at the most crucial times. But they did learn that responding to Christ's call was for real. They certainly understood that, if they were to be disciples, it was necessary to make a daily, fresh renewal of devotion and loyalty to Jesus Christ.

Those early disciples found the Christian life to be the most meaningful and rewarding way to live. They came to understand and personally experience the fact that there finally was an answer to evil, injustice, and sin. They realized that in Jesus there was forgiveness now, hope for the future, and the ultimate triumph of God.

The first disciples also shared the good news of what they had experienced. They told what had happened to them. They brought other people to Jesus. They invited others to join them in their commitment to Christ. They responded creatively to the Lord's commands, "Follow me" and "Go ye."

Here, then, is discipleship. It is *responding* to Christ's call. It is *following* Christ's way of life. It is *sharing* Christ with others. It is *committing* one's all to Christ.

Think through this joyful testimony of the most eminent

disciple concerning his evaluation of what it means to be a disciple. "Not only those things; I reckon everything as complete loss for the sake of what is so much more valuable, the knowledge of Christ Jesus my Lord. For his sake I have thrown everything away; I consider it all as mere garbage, so that I might gain Christ, and be completely united with him. No longer do I have a righteousness of my own, the kind to be gained by obeying the Law. I now have the righteousness that comes from God, and is based on faith. All I want is to know Christ and experience the power of his resurrection; to share in his sufferings and become like him in his death, in the hope that I myself will be raised from death to life" (Phil. 3:8-11, TEV).

Remembering that Paul was not only the most diligent disciple but the most persecuted one as well, isn't it an evidence of the quality of his discipleship that he could pen the epistle of joy (Philippians) which erupts with rejoicing at least eighteen times?

Jesus said, "If anyone wants to follow in my footsteps, he must give up all right to himself, take up his cross and follow me" (Mark 8:34, Phillips). This statement contains the meaning of discipleship, the measure of discipleship, and the motive for discipleship.

Sunday School teachers who are themselves experiencing the joy of discipleship are likely the best equipped persons to help others know the joy of becoming a disciple. And when they look back over the year, the decade, or a lifetime and see persons whom they have taught giving evidence of their own discipleship, that is real joy in its fullest.

Rejoice in Disciples Becoming Leaders

Discipleship begins in the act of conversion and reconciliation with God. But discipleship is more than a once-

in-a-lifetime experience. It is, in fact, a continuing experience throughout a lifetime. There is a natural law which operates in growth. Few, if any, living things come into the world fully grown. There are stages of development. If the growth pattern for some reason is blocked, the results are disastrous. The normal and typical growth is, however, a beautiful phenomenon of God's creative genius.

Jesus used the analogy of the rebirth to explain how a person becomes something new, a disciple. But a disciple must grow and mature. That is the essence of his nature. Discipleship which has been born in a genuine experience of salvation and is properly nourished grows inevitably toward maturity unless something blocks the growth. Growth and maturity are not ends. They are means. They are the means for serving Christ and his kingdom. To fail at this point of service is to fall short of being a disciple, no matter how knowledgeable a Christian may be.

When an individual has become a true disciple, his discipleship is observable. For example, a person may become more truthful and less inclined to "embellishment." Another may become more accepting and less judgmental. Another may become more thoughtful and less demanding. Yet another may become more generous and less selfish. And still another may become more spiritually minded and less carnal.

But an even more exciting sign of growth is seen when some members become officers and teachers in the Sunday School, and others go on to become deacons or church leaders in some other special capacity. Some may even respond to a call to a church-related vocation. These developments are highly regarded signs of discipleship. But there are other important evidences that a disciple has become a leader. All members should become responsible Christian leaders in their business, social, and civic life. All of these evidences of growth, maturity, and meaningful discipleship are cause for joy unlimited.

But one of the most superb joys is often overlooked. It is that personal exultation that comes from this realization: In the process of helping others become what God wants them to become, you yourself have been growing, maturing, and becoming what God wants you to become! When this exciting realization comes home to you, you cannot fail to "Rejoice, You're a Sunday School Teacher."

But, there is still another magnificent joy awaiting. It is not the joy of what you have taught. It is not the joy of seeing the fruits of your teaching. It is not the reward that you will eventually receive. It is the joy of seeing Christ who has saved, called, and enabled you to help make disciples. And when your earthly time of serving him is over, the ultimate joy will just have started. Anticipate, if you can, just what his indescribable "welcome home" and his divine commendation: "Well done, thou good and faithful servant" (Matt. 25:21) will be like!

And that, dear teacher, will truly be joy unlimited. It will be "joy unspeakable and full of glory" (1 Pet. 1:8).

About the Author

DR. JOHN T. SISEMORE is Director, Sunday School Division of the Baptist General Convention of Texas. He is recognized in the Southern Baptist Convention and also among other denominations for his expertise in the area of Sunday School/Bible teaching work.

Before going to Texas, he served as an adult consultant and as supervisor of the adult field services section, Sunday School Department of the Baptist Sunday School Board, Nashville, Tennessee.

His prior ministry includes director of the Department of Religious Education for the Oregon-Washington Baptist Convention (seven years) and minister of education in Texas churches (sixteen years).

He is a native of Oklahoma and is married to the former Margaret Lois Dornhoefer.

He is the author of many books in the field of religious education and Sunday School work, including this book and *Blueprint for Teaching*, Broadman release, and *The Ministry of Visitation*, Convention Press.

Dr. Sisemore has studied at Multnomah College, Moody Bible Institute, Chicago Music College, and Southern Baptist Seminary. He also holds the honorary Litt.D. degree.